HEART OF STONE

DRAMA

Kraftgriots

Also in the series (DRAMA)

HEART OF STONE

DRAMA

Ahmed Yerima

kraftgriots

Published by

Kraft Books Limited
6A Polytechnic Road, Sango, Ibadan
Box 22084, University of Ibadan Post Office
Ibadan, Oyo State, Nigeria
℗ 0803 348 2474, 0805 129 1191
E-mail: kraftbooks@yahoo.com

© Ahmed Yerima, 2013

First published 2013

ISBN 978–978–918–126–1

= KRAFTGRIOTS =
(A literary imprint of Kraft Books Limited)

All Rights Reserved

First printing, June 2013

DEDICATION

This play is dedicated to all those who have lost their lives in the various religious uprisings in Nigeria.

AUTHOR'S NOTE

I am not sure if I achieved what I wanted with this play. I wanted to raise a number of issues; the strength of beliefs, the disrespect to life, becoming heretical about the sociocultural things we hold dear, and how easy it is to sever the interlinks of lives in contemporary times.

The new reality in my country constantly confuses me. The insecurity contrasts so well with our search for the meaning of new and more peaceful existence, and our place within our own new modernity. I shall pause here. The story is a sad tale and yet real. Sadder still are the characters, because they all live next to us.

For this one play, I shall thank God, life ... and death. The opposing forces of existence.

Ahmed Yerima,
Mowe.

DRAMATIS PERSONAE

Kaka Patu
Achief
Amina
Musa
Kaka Vero
Gladys
Miri
Pastor Solomon
Wade
Ali
Sheik Sani
Tingi
Sargent
Kadia
People

When lights come on, two elders are seated, old man ACHIEF *on a mat, and old woman* KAKA PATU *on a small stool in* ACHIEF's *room.*

PATU: For seven nights now, I have continued to have the same nightmare. I see my daughter, Seluma, crying. (*Pause.*) By Allah, her tears were wet, colourless and real. So sad they wet the edges of her white shroud. Why would a ghost cry? I thought she was beyond all that now? Remember how we were told as children that the feelings of the dead died with them. No, not my child, not Seluma. (*Pause.*) Her eyes were swollen, red and wet, just the way they were before she died. The whole dream is so real, it frightens me. It is when I awake that the emptiness returns. The pains all return ... in triple folds ... eighteen years ago, as if it was yesterday. What is all this? What have I done? I pray five times a day, and yet I cannot find a clue. Everything is lost to me. (*Pause as she sobs quietly.*)

ACHIEF: Woman, talk to me please!

PATU: (*Clears her throat as she finds a voice.*) Maybe ... I ... have ... Have I failed her again? I know the circumstances with which she left this world was sad and sudden, but it was a long time ago. I have not slept a wink since then without a thought of her ... And each time I see her son, Musa, I feel fulfilled, but why does she still cry as if we left her legacy unattended? Why? (*Cries for a while.*)

ACHIEF:(*Shakes his head.*) Stop, woman. It is alright. I hate it when women cry. You cannot hear a thing.

PATU: (*Stops her cry. Stares at nothing and later wipes her tears.*) That is why I have come to see you, Achief. You are the eldest man in the family. (*Begins to cry again.*) If there is something to be done beyond prayers … an atonement to appease the soul of my late daughter. Or anything I left undone, to let her rest better, I want it done immediately. I can raise some money if things are needed. (*Breaks down.*)

ACHIEF: Yes, remind me. How did your daughter die?

PATU: Childbirth. She bled to death.

ACHIEF: The child?

PATU: Musa. He lives. The borehole digger, remember? Haa, Papa, you forget your own son?

ACHIEF: Um! A borehole digger. That is a very hard work.

PATU: Yes. As a borehole digger. But he brings life to the village, and all the other villages.

ACHIEF: An earth digger with blistered palms, and sore feet! Um! That is the small boy you gave my father's big traditional title to?

PATU: Ha … I had prayed this would not come up. My late husband, your brother, had said this as his last wish. He wanted Musa to be the Daudu after him. He said your father had said …

ACHIEF: Were you there? By Allah, I thought they said no woman was present in the room when he breathed his last?

PATU: Yes … there were the Mallams who came to pray

for his soul to be accepted by Allah as he died. He had spoken with them. Asking in clear words that they tell me, the Magajia, to make sure that his grandson by my daughter became Daudu after him. He even scribbled it and left the sheet of paper between his Quran. The last wish of a dying man is like an order from God himself.

ACHIEF: And so before my brother's body was cold, even before he was put in the grave, you rushed his grandson to the king and wrapped his small innocent head with a title meant for elders. (*Chuckles*.) A mere child!

PATU: I am sorry ... I thought ...

ACHIEF: And I heard that you have even gone and sold my brother's prime land by the stream which I wanted. That one in Angwa Rimi, on Abdulkadir Street. Not even in Kawo *fa*! I told you that I wanted that land, but you could not wait to deny me the only inheritance I wanted from my brother.

PATU: Yes, you told me, but we needed the money for Musa's school fees.

ACHIEF: (*Raises his voice*.) Who said he had to go to school? Who?

PATU: I.

ACHIEF: Always you. Woman, that land was ...

PATU: *Na maman shi mana*. His mother's land, not your brother's. The land initially belonged to my mother, who made it over to my daughter. She only allowed her father, my husband, your brother to farm there. When both my husband and my daughter died, I became hard up, no helper, and Musa was eager to learn. I knew and felt it was the right thing to do at the time. If he had grown up a Koranic teacher, he would have been ten times better than a borehole digger. *(Cries again.)* You only need to see his blistered palms. I oil them every night.

ACHIEF: Um. So what do you want me to do for you now? Since you know everything.

PATU: Forgive me.

ACHIEF: *A to*!

PATU: Help me. Tell me that all will be well. You are our father now. The main rock of the family house. Forgive my mistakes, old one.

ACHIEF: Um! Woman ... I am not ... one of the ancestors yet, just the oldest man in the village and head of our family. Part of my task as the oldest man is to take messages of the living to the dead. But we just did the normal offerings, and gave the ancestors all they asked for, two chickens, and a big keg of *burukutu*. Abukeli, the family priest, said they were happy, and we are all covered by their protection and blessings. So, go home, all is and will be well.

PATU: But not with my daughter. She is not happy. And I suppose now dead, she is one of our ancestors.

ACHIEF: Is she? You cannot say that. She was a daughter in this family. A mere vessel. But she tried, at least she gave us a son.

PATU: So, my daughter does not qualify? Now she is just a common vessel, even though she is buried in your ancestral land. The family black stone rests on her grave like any other member of this family, but she is not an ancestor. She cannot share in the goat they eat and wet her throat with the *burukutu* offerings because she is just a common dead woman vessel.

ACHIEF: Ah ah! I did not say so. There you go again, putting words in my mouth. All I said is that ...

PATU: No wonder she cried like a baby in my dreams, her shroud stained, cheated even in the land of the dead. No wonder!

ACHIEF: Woman, you try my patience ... You always do this to me. Who are you to speak so ill of the dead in such a foul manner? Are you Abukeli? Are you now the family priest?

PATU: No ... but ...

ACHIEF: Then keep to your part of your family duties. You are our wife. (PATU *begins to sob*.) Why are you crying again? When your husband died, I told you to take one of his brothers and marry him. Did you?

PATU: You were the only brother left by my late husband. The only one he had. I could not marry you. We were all too closely related. You were like my brother. Marrying you would have been like throwing a stone of discord into the family. Your wives were my sisters.

ACHIEF: Heaven knows how you know these stupid things you say. You felt too good for me, so you interpreted our tradition to suit your selfish purpose. See what you have become. A wasted, spent old widow, untouched, crying all over the place seeing ghosts in broad daylight. Um!

PATU: No!

ACHIEF: The gods bear me witness. All I wanted to do was help you. Your grandson was a handful even at the time. You were too old to bring him up all by yourself. What did I need you for? Sleep? I have three wives of my own. I only felt sorry for you. Apart from your skill at making good *burukutu*, my brother, God rest his soul, left nothing in you for any man. Yet you refused me. And you told the whole world how I pestered you. Me? When your daughter died at childbirth I was there for you. Was I not? Hm? Speak! (PATU *nods her head in agreement*.) But you continued to treat me with disdain. Now all old and spent, you run to me to tell me how you saw your late daughter crying in your dream. How will she not cry? When she sees you drying up like an old twig meant for firewood? Please nothing is wrong with anybody. The ancestors are happy. As the head of the family, I speak with them through the priest each market day. (PATU *kneels*.) What is this?

PATU: I am sorry.

ACHIEF: You should be sorry for yourself, old woman. All this is late now. I take a new wife to complete

14

the number Allah approved for me as a good Muslim soon. What can I possibly do with you now? *(Looks at her for a while.)* Anyway, I forgive you, I shall ask Abukeli about your worries in seven day's time.

PATU: Seven days?

ACHIEF: Yes. That is when the ancestral masquerade shall come out to dance once again. That is when I speak with them. Do you have any reservation?

PATU: No ... I am happy now. Thank you. *(Unties her wrapper and takes out some money which she hands to him.* ACHIEF *collects it.)* Kaka ...

ACHIEF: Um!

PATU: There is still the issue of my missing grandson. He has not been home for six weeks.

ACHIEF: I say you have the heart of a stone. A big crude uncut stone. The type used to block the deep gullies at Tudun Wada. Six whole weeks, you lost our son, but instead you came here to tell me of a stupid dream about the ghost of your daughter crying. How will she not cry? Um?

PATU: At first I thought it was alright. He's grown up now. But six weeks and not a word is too much even for a grown-up. That got me worried.

ACHIEF: How about Kadiri's daughter?

PATU: Amina?

ACHIEF: Yes. The nurse. Surely, she must know of his

whereabouts. They are always together.

PATU: Haa, Baba ... so you see them?

ACHIEF: Why not? I have eyes. I see them always on his *achaba* riding all over town. She clinging to him so tightly as if her life depends on the hold. Um! *(Thinks for a while.)* No. He must be alright. Abukeli must have known. He would have told me. I am sure he ran away from the stranglehold of the two women in his life. *(Chuckles.)* You need to see that girl cling on to him. *(He gets up.)* I think I can check on that myself. *(Goes into a room, and returns.)* He is well. He will return as fit as a fiddle soon.

PATU: Soon? *(Pause.)* And so easy?

ACHIEF: Yes. What do you think? That we need a megaphone to speak with the gods? Um! Today, soon. Go home. He shall return today.

(Lights slowly fade.)

Lights come on to reveal a sitting room. It is sparsely decorated. When lights come on, MUSA, *a young man with an unkempt beard is eating and* AMINA *is doting on him.* MUSA *is cold, speaks with a controlled amount of anger. He snaps at her once in a while which brings fear to the eyes of* AMINA.

MUSA: Water! Woman, quick!

AMINA: *(Offstage.)* I am coming. I cannot find the water in the fridge. Just bottles of *burukutu*.

MUSA: Under the bed! Kaka never puts water in the fridge! Check the big cloth bag under the bed. Woman! *(Continues to cough.)* I shall be dead by the time you arrive. Move! On the double. *(He continues coughing.)*

AMINA: *(Comes in holding two sachets of 'pure water'.)* Move on the double? Where did you learn this new awful language from? You sounded like the Zuma masquerade. With its frightening guttural voice fit only for the worship of the stone god. Ha ... Musa, you have become so impatient! By Allah, where did you learn all this?

MUSA: *(He gets up. Goes to her and collects one sachet from her forcefully, after a little struggle from her. He puts his teeth on the edge and in one gulp pulls out the water, drinks and emptys it. Panting.)* You will kill me if I do not watch it. *(He returns to the chair and continues eating.)*

AMINA: *(She stands, watching him as he eats, shaking her head sadly.)*

17

MUSA: *(Looks up.)* What?

AMINA: *(In a whisper.)* Nothing. I just don't know this man anymore.

MUSA: Who?

AMINA: You!

MUSA: Oh, woman! *(He takes the second sachet of water, empties it. He takes out a stick of cigarette and lights it. AMINA stares at him in disbelief. MUSA moves to her and blows the smoke in her face, she begins to cough. AMINA runs to her bag and takes out an inhaler to her nose. MUSA does not move, he just stares at her.)* I am sorry.

AMINA: *(Clears her throat.)* No, you are not. There you are standing like an effigy. God, I must leave. You don't need me here. *(She picks up her bag and begins to walk to the door. MUSA stops her.)* You know where to find me if and when you want me.

MUSA: *(As she steps away, MUSA grabs her, and they hug. She struggles a little.)* I am sorry. I really am very sorry. Please, forgive me. I am sorry. By Allah I am.

AMINA: Leave me alone. I swear, I don't know you anymore. Right from when you came to the hospital. With that funny bag on your back. I did not recognize you at first because of the beard. *(She breaks the embrace.)* Six weeks, and no one knew where you were. I cried all night. I thought something bad had happened to you. You just came with that stupid friend of yours to the hospital and told me that you had found a solution to our money problem.

MUSA: Zakari!

AMINA: Yes, him. I hate him. He frightens me. He looks straight through at people, with his stone-cold eyes. I told you to leave him alone. But no. That day, grinning from ear to ear, you said you were travelling to Katsina, that you had found a job. I tried to persuade you not to go, but he just stood there with a cold knowing smile. The type people give when they know they have won an argument. He never said a word, just that stupid smile. In a flash, you were gone. Choosing Zakari over and above me and your grandmother.

MUSA: It is okay. At least I am back.

AMINA: With Zakari?

MUSA: No. I came back alone. We went our separate ways. I left him in er ... in the ... (*Goes to her.*) Amina, I am sorry. See I am here now. To stay with you and Kaka Patu forever.

AMINA: Again you lie.

Musa: I swear!

AMINA: (*Still crying.*) I missed you with every bone of my body. The villagers had started to jeer. My father had started making arrangements to marry me off to Aliyu Danbata in Birnin Gwari. Thank your stars you returned today. They come for my hand tomorrow.

MUSA: All nonsense. I am back. See. *(Runs to his bag, brings out a small pouch.)* See. *(Shows her money.)* Money. All for our wedding.

AMINA: Are you sure?

MUSA: More than life itself. I went to work. To make some money for us. How many boreholes do we need to feed you and our children?

AMINA: Children?

MUSA: Yes ... all ten of them ... *(They both chuckle.)* This was why I had to leave. Here ... now you keep it. This way you will trust me more. Take it.

AMINA: I should? There is still the matter of the baby.

MUSA: Baby? Which baby?

AMINA: Mine. Ours, yours ...

MUSA: Allah be praised! Now we have nine more to go. See I am no longer afraid of fear. At first I lived in despair ... afraid of tomorrow. Now Allah has answered our prayers. Does Kaka know?

AMINA: No. I wanted you ... us to tell her. Oh, I am so happy. I was afraid that you would reject me ... or even reject it. Where was I going to go?

MUSA: Aliyu's house in Birnin Gwari.

AMINA: I swear I had made up my mind to kill myself. *(Pause.)* But how did you know?

MUSA: I suspected.

AMINA: You did? How?

MUSA: I just knew. Your eyes told me.

AMINA: How?

MUSA: That day, as you cried and missed me. You cried for two people. It was in your eyes.

AMINA: Ha …by Allah … you are wicked. You disappeared, and it all looked so hopeless. But today Allah's smiles are on me. On us. Hold me close one more time. Oh, Musa, I missed you.

MUSA: By Allah, I missed you, too! All is well now. My new employers promised us a good life. Take the money home to your place and hide it. Now, Amina!

AMINA: (AMINA *collects it*.) Ha, it is heavy.

MUSA: It is a lot of money. Hurry, go and hide it. If well invested, all your dream of leaving the smelly hospital cleaner's job will come true. Our son will also have a good future.

AMINA: A son? How do you know it is a son?

MUSA: It is the blessed prayer of my forefathers. All our wives have sons as their first children. Yours won't be different. By Allah, it won't.

AMINA: *Amin*. And Aliyu Danbata and his stupid wedding?

MUSA: I shall see your brother this evening. Tomorrow, we shall give your mother all the money she needs to buy the *kayan awure*. Your bridal load must be the best in the village. Now hurry, pack all the things home and wait for me.

AMINA: Yes ... yes ... (*As she packs her gifts into the bag.*) Tell Kaka that I was here. I left her food in the kitchen. Her medication is under her pillow.

MUSA: Her medication?

AMINA: Her feet got worse in your absence. Sometimes the pains gave her fainting spells. She must rest after taking the drugs. Please, tell her.

MUSA: I will. I hear footsteps. Take the back door. I shall come to your house later. Hurry. (*They hug. AMINA runs out.*) Now the night owl is out. Allah forgive me!

(*The door opens slowly. MUSA runs behind the door. KAKA PATU enters opening the door slowly. She walks into the room. Turns around wondering.*)

PATU: I can smell my grandson. I know you are here. My nostrils perceive you. Out, Son!

MUSA: (*He jumps out from the back of the door, trying to startle KAKA PATU.*) Pooh!

PATU: (*She lets out a little yell.*) Hao! You caught me, Son. You must hug the baby monster now. (*They hug lovingly.*) Oh, I have missed you, Son. No matter how big you are, you are still my baby boy.

MUSA: Yes, Kaka.

PATU: Turn around for the baby monster, or I will pull your cheeks until they tear to shreds. (*She pulls his cheeks.*) They have gone both bearded, Son. Hm, you have lost some weight. I must make sure you eat.

MUSA: Food, Kaka?

PATU: Yes, food. You had me worried, Son. Six weeks. You should have at least sent a word. I started having nightmares. The ghost of your mother came to ask me where I had sent you.

MUSA: My mother? She has been dead like forever.

PATU: I know. But she came into my dream crying. Calling your name all the time. You got me really scared, Son. So I went to see Kaka Achief.

MUSA: Kaka Achief? To tell him what?

PATU: To tell him I had lost you.

MUSA: And what did he say?

PATU: What else? He said a lot of things, and said nothing. But he wants to see you.

MUSA: Me? Whatever for?

PATU: To scold you. It is good you came. You must hurry to him. Vero's daughter, Gladys is getting married soon. They are bringing the husband to meet me. I need you to buy some bottled drinks. They may not all be able to drink *burukutu*. But first your uncle. When you see him, listen more, talk less, you hear?

MUSA: Yes … yes, Kaka. (*Hurries to his second bag, takes out a bundle of wrapper, and an envelope.*) Here, for you, Kaka.

PATU: For me? (*She opens the envelope first.*) Money!

MUSA: Quick, Kaka hide this. It is for the rainy day like you used to say. Whatever happens, tell no one about this?

PATU: What can happen, Son?

MUSA: Nothing, Kaka. Ha, you look frail. How about your feet?

PATU: They still hurt, Son. Sometimes I cannot walk, I just sit and stay at home. Thank God for Amina. Now that you are back, we must hurry with your wedding arrangements, I am hearing funny stories about other suitors. And she is a good girl.

MUSA: Yes ... yes, Kaka.

PATU: See the miracle of God. You have brought money. *(Serious.)* It is good money, Son?

MUSA: I worked for it. Good clean money. I never want you to know poverty again or sell anymore properties. I am back now, I shall do all the things expected of a man. (KAKA PATU *unties her wrapper, and unzips the pocket of her little inner skirt, she drops the envelope and ties her wrapper back.)* Good.

PATU: Ha! My son. May Allah bless you. *(Then she unwraps the bundle, and two wrappers fall out.)* Huh! *Maganan kayan aure.* Our dresses for the wedding! God bless you, Son. How did you know, Son? Kaka Vero and I needed something special to wear for Gladys' wedding. *(She hugs him.)*

MUSA: *(Brings out another bundle. Gives it to her.)* This one, Kaka, do not open it until I tell you when. It is for a special occasion.

PATU: Can I take a peep, Son? I am dying to see it. What colour is it, Son? I am sure it is for your wedding. Haa!

MUSA: I will tell you when. Keep it safe, Kaka.

PATU: With my life. By Allah, I am so happy. All these for me? *(She hugs him again.)* Thank you for buying something for Kaka Vero.

MUSA: I knew that if I didn't you would have killed me.

PATU: Yes, I would have. She is my twin sister, remember? *(She starts a song and begins to dance. MUSA joins her as lights slowly go off.)*

Lights come on to reveal ACHIEF's *house. He sits on the rug, excited. Gifts bought for him by* MUSA *are on the rug.* MUSA *sits watching him.*

ACHIEF: Now with this beard, and red deep set eyes, you remind me of Garuba, your great-grandfather, my own father. Fearsome warrior, that one. *(Pause.)* Until his death, he never liked your father.

MUSA: Why? How can a man have two sons and love one more? You were like a pair of twins. Same father and mother, by Allah, what kind of a man was my great-grandfather that he would select even among his blood, who to love?

ACHIEF: A great man of war. His temper like wildfire could burn down a whole village in a second. He thrived only when he had wars to fight, and when the wars ended, and the white men came with their laws, he did not know what to do.

MUSA: So he took to drinking?

ACHIEF: Yes. And merriment. All night he would drink, sing and dance, and all day he would sleep. A typical warrior's life.

MUSA: My grandfather?

ACHIEF: Your grandfather on the other hand was a man of peace. Our father never understood why.

MUSA: Hm. Great-grandfather must have been a handful like Zuberu's father.

ACHIEF: Yes. But he was never stupid with his own. He

could drink two kegs of *burukutu* and still return home on his own. We never picked him from the houses of his friends or the palace like most drinkers.

MUSA: Ha … so that is what happened?

ACHIEF: Yes.

MUSA: Warrior! I always wondered how he lost his last two fingers on his left hand.

ACHIEF: War. (*Pause. Then slowly begins to laugh.*)

MUSA: What?

ACHIEF: My great father was wonderful in death more than life. He had an uncanny power to predict what would happen days before they would, and he was always right.

MUSA: Really? I wish …

ACHIEF: Every man who has Garuba's blood running in his veins inherited it. It is a frightening power to possess though. (*Laughs again.*)

MUSA: Uncle, what?

ACHIEF: Five days before he died. He woke up, packed all his personal property in his room into two big bundles. Just before the first cock crowed. Then he got all the women in the household to bring their children to his room, where he taught them a song. He now invited your grandfather and I to his room, where we met you sitting on his lap, his royal red Daudu's hat on your little head. He made us promise to get the children sing that song as we take him into the big bush for his burial on a rainy day in five days time. He also requested that two gunshots be fired, each by us, before he would be taken into the big bush.

MUSA: What did you do?

ACHIEF: What could we do? We were torn between laughter and seriousness, especially when he said that failure to carry out his wishes would lead to the death of his first son immediately after his death.

MUSA: Ha, Great-grandfather.

ACHIEF: And I would lead a wasted life losing the title of Daudu to you.

MUSA: Me? A baby?

ACHIEF: We laughed it off. The man was drunk we told ourselves. He was a year over a hundred years old. Frail and very fair skinned, bearded like you are now. We just nodded, laughed and returned to our wives.

MUSA: Hm. This is what I missed about village life, everything appears so simple. Big problems explained away with one little story.

ACHIEF: (*Chuckles.*) Yes. But exactly five days after, he died.

MUSA: He did?

ACHIEF: *Kwarai*! Like he had said he would. It also

rained non-stop like he had also said it would. In our grief, we forgot to gather the children to sing. We even forgot the gunshots. But as we carried him to the entrance of the big bush, the necks of the three men who carried his body turned. And without a word they returned home, propelled by a spirit we could not see.

MUSA: Ha. What did you do?

ACHIEF: Dumbfounded, we followed, angered more by the delay in laying our father to his final rest.

MUSA: Hm.

ACHIEF: Indeed. It was when we got home, and they laid him back on his creaky bamboo *karaga*, with a smugness on his wet face, shaped out by the wetness of his shroud, that we remembered his words.

MUSA: What did you do then?

ACHIEF: We gathered the children, and they sang. Your grandfather and I shot a round of our guns each, and we buried him.

MUSA: Good.

ACHIEF: But ...

MUSA: But ... *(Realizes slowly.)* My grandfather ...

ACHIEF: He died ten years after. And I lost my Daudu title to you.

MUSA: Allahu-Akbar!

ACHIEF: So, when your grandmother came here to say

you had been missing for six weeks, I was very worried.

MUSA: Worried? Why? I was fine. See I am fine.

ACHIEF: Yes, I can see. I even thank you for these lovely gifts. But I am still worried.

MUSA: Why?

ACHIEF: My father, your great-grandfather, had said that you would not live long. And if care was not taken, you would die a very violent death. Abukeli and I made sacrifices. But I wonder now if our ancestors can change it now. He kept seeing you in a pool of blood. Your limbs torn apart. Your heart spitting bloody pellet of stones. I have not slept a wink since then, Son.

MUSA: A warrior's death then? *(Suddenly cheerful. Excited.)* Like him?

ACHIEF: Oh you speak like a child, Son. I speak of life, and you embrace death. Just who are you? Where did you go, Son? Tell me so that we can ask our ancestors to let the mark of death pass over you. Son, where did you go?

MUSA: To where boys become men. To where the brain is washed. Where the heart is transfixed and the eyes focused.

ACHIEF: To heaven then?

MUSA: A place sweeter than heaven, life is perfect and everyone is happy.

ACHIEF: A dream land then. No, this is not our lot. There they planted in your heart, a stone, a chip off the Zuma rock. Your eyes burn with the anger of a ... Oh my god!

MUSA: Kaka Achief, have I ever asked you for a favour?

ACHIEF: Always. Why do you think they call me your uncle? That is my punishment from Allah. Hm. A burden I gladly bear. What now? What do you want?

MUSA: If anything happens to me, please take care of Kaka Patu and Kaka Vero.

ACHIEF: Your two mothers.

MUSA: Yes. Will you?

ACHIEF: I have no choice, do I? (*Pause. Watches* MUSA *for a while.*) Alright I will.

MUSA: Good, Kaka Achief, when you look at me, what do you see?

ACHIEF: I see death ... just like they did.

MUSA: Who? (*Pause.*) Who did? Who saw what, Uncle?

ACHIEF: Garuba my father and Abukeli ... our family priest. They saw death. (*In a whisper.*) And I fear ...

MUSA: Kaka Achief, a death that has meaning is good. Did Great-grandfather and Abukeli see a hero's death for me?

ACHIEF: Hooo! Hooo! (*Pauses for a while.*)

MUSA: Hm? Speak to me, Kaka Achief!

ACHIEF: (*Whispers.*) Not quite. But out of this stupid village story, please find some sense in it, son.

MUSA: (*Stares at him for a while.*) Hm!

(*Slowly lights go off.*)

When lights come on, MUSA *is on his prayer mat, praying.* KAKA PATU *knocks the door.* MUSA *does not answer. He only claps. The door opens slowly,* KAKA PATU *comes in, head covered crying.* MUSA *is shocked, but continues the last part of the prayer.*

PATU: If that is the prayer that you have been praying to Allah, then may he not listen to you.

MUSA: Kaka, what you have just done is *haram*. I was praying. I may have to say my prayers again.

PATU: Say it a hundred times, and two hundred times over, Allah shall not listen or answer your prayers. *(She begins to cry loudly.)*

MUSA: Kaka, kill me at home, do not take me to the market square. I beg you. Hush! How do we explain your tears at this time of the morning?

PATU: The way I will explain your prayers to the neighbours at the early hours of the morning. *(She kneels down.)*

MUSA: *(Shocked, kneels too.)* Kaka, I beg you get up. Kaka!

PATU: Then tell me what I have done wrong. Why would a young man who is hale and healthy, virile and strong, say prayers meant for funeral all by himself? Today is the seventh day that you have done this. Why, Son? Are you sick? Is there something I should know?

MUSA: There is nothing, Kaka. I just felt like saying the prayers.

PATU: That Allah should receive your soul? Forgive you your sins? Forgive your iniquities and accept you in *Aljenah? (She cries louder.)* You lie, Son! *Karia. Ka dena karia.* Not this way! *Walahi,* not this way!

MUSA: Don't cry, Kaka. Tears are a waste of precious water, especially when the heart is made of stone. I was only praying for my mother's soul, and maybe mine. Praying and hoping that time will once again pass quickly.

PATU: Your mother's soul? The *janaiza?* A funeral prayer for a woman long dead and buried? *Sallah gawa?* Son, please!

MUSA: Yes.

PATU: But she died the day you were born. And I have prayed for her soul since then, Musa. We have watched you with fear in our hearts.

MUSA: We?

PATU: Yes, we.

MUSA: I shall kill Amina when I see her.

PATU: Not Amina. Your mother and I. She woke me up. The same dream, crying, her shroud wrapped around her. Only this time, she held another one. At first I thought it was for me, so I stretched my hand to collect it. But she shook her head, as another hand came from behind me to collect it. When I turned my face, it was yours I saw, Musa. Yours. We both started to cry in the dream, as she begged me to hurry to you. But here you are, Musa, a living corpse! Why?

MUSA: My mother did and said all that?

PATU: Yes. She does not want to see you now. I am supposed to go before you. That is how it should be. Who will bury me? What did you give me this for? *(In one swift move, she takes out the money* MUSA *gave her and throws it on the prayer mat. She hurries out and returns with the bundle of wrapped cloth.)* I don't want this either. *(On second thought she takes it and unwraps it. It is a white bundle of cloth. She lets out a loud yell.)* It is an *likaffani*! You have even bought your own shroud. By Allah! Musa, you have killed me! *(She faints.)*

MUSA: *(Panics as he goes on his knees trying to attend to her, there is a knock on the door. Slowly* AMINA *opens the door and walks in.)*

AMINA: *Ina ku anah*! I am on my way to the hospital, I thought I should make breakfast for tying your fast.

(Slowly lights go off.)

KAKA PATU's *living room. When lights come on,* KAKA VERO, KAKA PATU *and* PASTOR *are seated.* GLADYS *and* MIRI *are on their knees.* AMINA *and* MUSA *watch while standing. They are singing and clapping.*

ALL: The God that answereth by fire!
     Let him be our God!
     The God that answereth by fire!
     Let him be our God!

KADIA: (*Moves forward to the centre as he signals the end of the song.*) Good evening, our mothers. I am the bringer of good news. Your daughter Gladys and our son Miri have decided to tie the wedding knot, and become one family. (*The others clap.*) We now invite Pastor Solomon who will be officiating at the wedding this Saturday, to lead us in prayer.

PASTOR: Praise the Lord!

ALL: Hallelujah!

PASTOR: Praise the living God!

ALL: Hallelujah!

PASTOR: Father Lord, we are here gathered in your name to bless the union between our son and our daughter. You are the God of love, so we beg you to bring love to their lives, keep them together in your name until death do them part. Grant us the grace of the event of Saturday. Let the wedding go unstopped, undestroyed, and unharmed. (*Starts a song, the others join.*)

Satan don fall for gutter!
March am!
March am!
Satan don fall for gutter!
March am!
March am!

(As the song goes into a frenzy, and the people dance wildly, an angry MUSA *walks out.* AMINA *runs after him. Lights go sharply off.)*

Outside the house. Spotlight. MUSA *stands angry.* AMINA *comes in.*

AMINA: Musa, why? Why did you leave that way? You got everybody worried.

MUSA: You heard the pastor. Didn't you?

AMINA: I did. But what did he say? It was a prayer, Musa. What is happening to you? Why?

MUSA: You heard the song? Didn't you?

AMINA: Yes, and what about it?

MUSA: Who do you think is the Satan who fell into the smelly gutter of hell?

AMINA: No one, just Satan. Musa, it is a song.

MUSA: A song, eh? Satan don fall for gutter. March am, march am. That's me. That's us. The song is saying that all Muslims are siblings of Satan, who should be trampled upon. We? Who did we ever hurt? I mean who are the peace-loving cursed docile illiterates? Us!

AMINA: Us?

MUSA: Yes … us Muslims. All their songs … all their prayers insult us. They brand us as the children of the most evil spirit, the devil. *Shetani*! They want hell fire to burn us to smithereens. And yet they want us to be one. To be friends. They say we worship the same God. How can? I swear I will not go for the wedding if this is the kind of songs they will sing at the wedding. Even their prayers are so militant, aimed at us described as blind 'gambari', beggar children of the devil.

(*From backstage, the sound of* KAKA VERO.)

AMINA: Kaka Vero wants you. Go to her. I am sure she is worried about your behaviour. Kaka Patu will be more worried. Go to her. Go to your mothers, Musa. Go!

MUSA: No!

VERO: There you are, Son. Amina, hurry to Kaka Patu, she needs you to serve the guests.

AMINA: Yes, Kaka. Musa, please. (*Exit.*)

VERO: I have not thanked you enough for the cloth you bought for your grandmother and I.

MUSA: There is no need, Kaka, *ba damua*. I did it for my mothers.

VERO: But you left suddenly. Six weeks, two days and eight hours.

MUSA: Haa … you counted, Kaka.

VERO: I did not. Gladys did. She counted every day of your absence. It reminded me of when you went to school to live in Rigan Chuku.

MUSA: Hm.

VERO: She cried every day, until you returned for holiday.

MUSA: Hm.

VERO: I saw that look in your eyes today. The very look you had in your eyes the day you were born. The look that made up my mind for me.

MUSA: What look, Kaka?

VERO: Find me something to sit. My legs ache.

MUSA: (MUSA *goes to a corner of the stage and brings an old plastic chair. KAKA VERO sits.*) I really must go in and join the rest.

VERO: Because you don't want to talk. Each time you don't want to say or do anything, you run away from the place or the people.

MUSA: Hm.

VERO: Or make those stupid short grunts that say more than we hear.

MUSA: I am sorry. It is out of respect really.

VERO: (*Chuckles.*) Moses ... I know you very well. (*Pause.*) Your mother died in my arms, you know?

MUSA: Kaka Patu told me.

VERO: Sometimes I want to say I killed her in order to give you life.

MUSA: Haa ... Kaka. Not tonight. Not now.

VERO: Did your grandmother tell you what happened on that day?

MUSA: A little.

VERO: A little is not enough. You need to know

everything. A fuller mouth with kolanut gives the fuller taste. I shall tell you all. So that you will know that we are one after all. Joined in tears and time. Entwined, Son. (*Clears her throat.*) When Gladys came home one rainy night crying, saying that you had broken off your engagement to her because she was your sister, I knew the reason was that you had become the pure believer and suddenly we had become filthy *kaffirs* to you. Yes? (*Pause.* MUSA *does not say a word.*)

MUSA: (*Clears his throat.*) Yes, Kaka.

VERO: The sad experience broke Gladys' heart. I sent her to live in Abuja with our relatives. And now she has been able to forget. She has met a man. Her type. Please, let her go.

MUSA: Yes, Kaka she can. I have no objections at all.

VERO: So when the prayers started, and you looked down at the kneeling couple and you walked out, I knew that knowing a little about how related we were was dangerous for the soul. I will not rest well in my grave if I don't tell you. Should I? Moses? Hm?

MUSA: Yes.

VERO: Gladys loves you.

MUSA: Like a brother. And I love her like a sister.

VERO: No. She became a sister as the last strand ... the last thing to hold on to when you became a teacher in a Koranic school, and suddenly we became dirty pigs ... unbelievers in your sight.

MUSA: Haa … Kaka!

VERO: Let me speak, Son. From the day I saw you as a little boy join a group of *Almajiri* to force a car driver to a stop and with your mouths you drew fuel from his car after beating him up for refusing to recite the *Fathia*; and as I watched, it first appeared like play to me. But in a frenzy of madness, you all ran towards our church, poured the petrol under the doors, while the other wild boys broke the church windows and threw in burning rags into it. Remember? As the church burnt, and the police and the Fire Brigade siren vehicles screamed and screeched, our eyes met, in one flash, I saw those red beady eyes of stone then, and you ran to the back door and carried me to safety. And everybody thought you were a hero. Remember? I would have died that day if God had not touched your heart.

MUSA: (*Kneels before her.*) I am sorry. It was what we were told to do. The *Ustaz* had said Allah had decreed it. We were used. First it started as a play, then it got out of hand. I'm sorry.

VERO: When my maternal cousin's house, Bitrus' house, was burnt in Koghum village in Wang District of Jos, with all five members of his family burnt alive, again it was another trip of madness? Millions have died after.

MUSA: I am sorry.

VERO: The very words the political and religious leaders said. They shook hands on television, hugged and swore to give us peace. We in turn trusted them.

Swept and washed all the blood and broken glasses away. We buried the dead, and shared their leftover children like inherited properties, ourselves not too sure of our tomorrow. As for you, what happened in our church, became our dark little secret. We have never spoken about it until tonight. But I always knew that there was some seething anger burning in you in your quietness. Your deceitful gentle nods. Your almost childlike amiable character. (*Pause.*) And what happened tonight ... (*Pause.*)

MUSA: Tonight? Yes, speak, Mother.

VERO: Confirmed my fears. As I watched you stare at us with those same eyes that saved me in the church hidden by the frightening beard, and the redness of your eyes, and as you looked at the pastor as he prayed, I knew that the playful madness was back again.

MUSA: Yes.

VERO: Your grandmother and I went through the civil war years together, you know? As widows, then friends and blood sisters. She has always been a Muslim, and I a Catholic, and each of us faced our God, until we got Him fused into one. We shared everything. When in Kano we heard of the butchering going on. Pregnant women slaughtered like Sallah rams at the abattoir, their unborn children yanked out, only to be strangled by the forced breath of life. I lost my twin sister in that madness. We, your grandmother and I, both agreed that it was a madness that would be over. It did. But these red eyes of yours frighten me.

MUSA: (*Chuckles again.*) My red eyes again. How come they have become a problem to those around me?

VERO: Because we know you. Because in them we see hatred for what we don't know. What we don't understand. (*Pause.*) And besides, I gave you life.

MUSA: You? *Wayo Allah na*! A ...

VERO: Yes ... a common Christian.

MUSA: Kaka, I did not mean it that way.

VERO: But your eyes spoke before your tongue could twist out the words. Your new stone-cold red eyes, innocent as an angel's pair of eyes, moved me to give you life.

MUSA: Hm. I don't understand.

VERO: Your mother was eight months pregnant. She had stayed at home that day refusing to go to work. I was in my shop when I heard a big bang coming from her room. She tried to take something which she had hidden in the ceiling, and she fell. There she was screaming for help. I ran in, and found her in a pool of blood. She had lost too much blood, and had started to pass away. Just then your grandmother came, and we decided to get you out. You had started to kick and fight for your life. And with the water broken, you had almost flowed out with it. The difficult decision was how to cut the umbilical cord. Your mother begged me to cut it close to her. If I did, she would die, and you would live. Being a midwife, and seeing how you wanted to live, I cut it close to her, unwrapped her breasts and made you suck them, until she went stiff cold. And when you continued to cry, I removed my withered breast and gave you.

MUSA: Mother ... I am sorry. I am so confused.

VERO: That is what life is all about. Elders pray for younger ones. May you not die young. And may you not see problems in life. (*Chuckles.*) The joke is one must choose one.

MUSA: I still don't understand.

VERO: (*Chuckles again.*) You have to live long in order to learn to endure problems. May you live long, Son. May the spirit of tolerance reign supreme in your now strong heart.

MUSA: Amen, Kaka.

VERO: Amen! Moses, you still remember!

MUSA: How can I forget? How you used to dress us up for church on Sunday. And we ate rice and chicken after church. I was Musa Mondays to Saturdays. And Moses only on Sundays. How can I possibly forget, Kaka?

VERO: Oh come, Moses, you are my son. Come to your second mother. (*They hug. She begins to cry.*) But now you hate me and my own. Why? (*She continues to cry, as* MUSA *hugs her.*) Anyway, whatever happens, this good times will remain with me forever.

MUSA: No. Nothing will happen to you, Kaka. I swear with my life.

VERO: *(Her hand to his lips.)* Ssh! *(In a whisper.)* Say it with your heart, Moses. Tell Musa. (GLADYS *comes out.*)

GLADYS: What is going on here? Kaka? Let him be. Uncle Tadoh cannot come tonight. So Kaka Patu wants Musa to stand in as my father, and now the pastor wants him to give the father's blessing for Miri and I.

MUSA: Me?

(Slowly MUSA and KAKA VERO look at GLADYS. MUSA rises, stretches his hands and hugs GLADYS. VERO joins them as lights slowly go off.)

Dark stage. Spotlight on the door. Front of KAKA PATU's *house. The door opens slowly.* MUSA *alights. He wears a jallabia. He holds a phone to his ear as he comes on stage.*

MUSA: Yes. I am in front of the house. You can take the stream path. It is lonely at this time. Alright, I shall wait outside. (*Switches off the phone.*) It is all happening so fast. I thought I would have some time to say my farewell. If only. If I could hold. No. I would have. No. I should have ... But no. By Allah, my mind wavers. Not now. Not me. Not here. Too late. (*A young man comes in with a big bag.*) Ali, you came.

ALI: (*Whispers.*) Ssh! No names. I did. Here. The stuffs are in the bag. (MUSA *tries to open the bag.*) What are you trying to do? We wear them only moments to the time.

MUSA: Do you know the target now?

ALI: No. They will call us on Saturday.

MUSA: Tomorrow? I thought ...

ALI: Don't think. We are not trained to think. Are you alright? Um? Remain focused on the course. (*He brings out a gun.*)

MUSA: A gun! Put the damn thing away, my grandmother sleepwalks.

ALI: Are you changing your mind? (*Coldly.*) Are you still with us?

MUSA: To the death. I say put the damn thing away. What is wrong with you?

ALI: No waver, um? Remember, the course is our respite. The great source of our hope for a change. A flash, a pinch, then perfect stillness and then heaven. Remember?

MUSA: Yes.

ALI: The *Suratuh* instructs us to defend ourselves against the infidels. The non-believers. Remember?

MUSA: Yes … but the Quran …

ALI: Then keep your mind focused. (*Pause.*) Maybe it was a bad idea to let you come home in the first place. Women! We should have kept you in the camp.

MUSA: No. I am fine! I am ready! I swear!

ALI: Don't let them get to you. Take the bag in and go to bed. See you tomorrow. Be prepared. You are getting me worried.

MUSA: No. Yes … yes, goodnight. (*Exit* ALI.) Tomorrow. Oh my God. What have I done? What do I tell Kaka Patu?

(*As* MUSA *carries the bag into the house, lights go off.*)

*There is the sound of an explosion in the darkness of the
stage. Sirens and voices of people at an incident is played
back. When lights come on,* KAKA PATU *is wearing her
dress for the wedding. She sits on a stool picking guinea
corn from a tray when* MUSA *runs in panting. When he
sees* KAKA PATU *blowing dirt from the corn, he is really
scared, and lets out a yell.* KAKA PATU *is shocked.*

MUSA: Kaka, you!

PATU: Yes, me.

MUSA: I thought you were in the church. I thought.

PATU: No. I dressed up to go, but my feet gave way. The
pain was killing. I took my drugs and slept off. When
I woke up, I felt it was too late to bother. I shall go
to the reception venue at the Town Council Hall. Or
better still, see them at home. But I have sent Agatha
with our gift.

MUSA: Yes. So you did not hear the bang then?

PATU: What bang? I slept off. Why are you so sweaty?
So finicky? So unsettled? Why? You did not go too?

MUSA: I did. But on the way, I ... met a dear old friend
on his way to Dutse, and I saw him off.

PATU: Dutse?

MUSA: Now I ... am suddenly very sick. I have a
headache, too. I want to rest. I do not wish to see
anyone. No one, Kaka, I beg you.

PATU: Then take one of my pills for headache. It will lift the head and wash off the ache clean. It is by my bedside. Two will do the job.

MUSA: Thank you, Kaka. (MUSA *hurries in. Unsure of what is wrong with* MUSA, *but visibly worried,* KAKA PATU *continues blowing the dirt off the guinea corn on the tray when* AMINA *runs in.*)

AMINA: (*Panting.*) Kaka, all hell has broken loose! They have blown it up!

PATU: Heaven help us. Another one! Where are you all running from?

AMINA: Thank God you are alive, Kaka. (*Breaks down and starts crying.*) Then they killed her. They killed them all. It was her, not you I saw! Eeooo!

PATU: They killed who? Stop crying woman and talk to me! Who?

AMINA: They bombed the church.

PATU: Oh woman. Which one?

AMINA: Everyone in the church was blown to their deaths. Kaka Vero, Gladys and her husband are all gone. Their blood splashed, their bodies Strewn in tiny bits and pieces were packed in different bags and brought to our hospital.

PATU: My sister, Vero, why?

AMINA: Who did they offend, Kaka? I say who? Who was so vexed that all these innocent people offended at once?

PATU: Ummm … my daughter, Gladys! What did they do to deserve such deaths?

AMINA: Headless bodies, Kaka, torn from limbs to limbs. We cannot even tell them apart. Why?

PATU: (KAKA PATU *watches as she speaks, the tray drops, as she slowly falls and faints.*)

AMINA: Then it is true. (*She cries louder.*) My Musa is also dead. Oh God what do I do now? (*As she rolls herself on the floor crying, the door slowly opens, and* MUSA *emerges. Sees him, she jumps on him.*) You are alive! Thank God!

MUSA: Yes, I have a headache, I could not go to the church. What is going on? (*Sees* KAKA PATU.) What happened to her?

AMINA: They killed them all. Two men came into the church. One ran as soon as he was identified, but the other man took off his jacket, screamed Allahu Akbar! And the whole church was blown to smithereens. Not one soul was spared.

MUSA: (*Aside.*) Allah, what have we done?

AMINA: Um? Kaka Vero, your second mother, is dead. Gladys and her husband died even before they could start their lives. I wept as I saw their hands cut off from their bodies still wearing their shining brand new rings. What a pitiful sight.

MUSA: You say someone saw the man who ran away?

AMINA: Yes. He is helping the police right now. They say he ran through the bush path towards the stream. May Allah deliver the evil man to the hands of the law. (KAKA PATU *begins to stir. She sits up slowly*.)

PATU: *Amin*! Whoever killed my sister shall not find peace even in death.

AMINA: He too must die. (KAKA PATU *still on the floor, sobs, staring at them*.) And you ... how did you escape?

MUSA: I ... er ... left on time to check on Kaka, I was worried when I did not see her in the church.

PATU: Um ... I thought your friend from Dutse came ...

MUSA: Kaka!

(*Just then two armed police men come in with a man who points at MUSA. MUSA attempts to run, but the policemen point their guns at him.*)

SARGENT: One step and you are dead. Please, come with us quietly. (MUSA *stops, the policemen handcuff him*.)

AMINA: No, what did he do?

PATU: He has been home with me. Let him be.

SARGENT: We just want to question him concerning the bombings at the church.

TINGI: I recognize him. He ran past me. We collided and I helped him up. His partner blew up the church.

AMINA: Musa, please say something.

MUSA: I am innocent. You shall see. I will soon be

52

home. (*The policemen take* MUSA *out.* TINGI *also exit.*)

PATU: Where is Musa going with those men? He has a headache.

AMINA: They have arrested him, Kaka, they think he has a hand in the killing of the people in Kaka Vero's church.

PATU: No. Musa cannot kill Vero. He calls her mother. (*Slowly she lies back.*) All this is becoming confusing. *Subahanallahi*! (*Faints again.*)

AMINA: No, Kaka not yet. Please, wake up. Not now. This is not the time. Musa is in big trouble.

(*As* AMINA *tries to revive her, lights slowly fade.*)

When lights come on, MUSA *is saying his prayers.* SHEIK SANI *comes in.* MUSA *whispers to the* WARDER *who tells him to wait. He continues to pray until he ends his prayers.*

SANI: To which God have you just prayed?

MUSA: To the one true God, Allah.

SANI: Then what are you doing here?

MUSA: Um?

SANI: What are you doing in prison, praying to the one true God? The Police Commissioner called me. He asked me to speak with you.

MUSA: As what? To get more information from the terrorist? At least that is the new name I am called. With that status, they have a right to my life.

SANI: Yes, they do. (*Pause.*) They also wanted to know if that is what I taught you in my Koranic school?

MUSA: And what did you say to them, Sheik? That you taught me all this?

SANI: I denied it vehemently ...

MUSA: You denied me, too.

SANI: Not so bluntly ... but yes. As a man of God, I have a lot at stake. As Chief Imam of the State, a lot of responsibility is placed upon my shoulders.

MUSA: (*Pause. Watches him for a while.*) I am sorry Sheik Sani ... my great teacher.

SANI: Amin. (*Pause. Looks at* MUSA.) What happened

to you? What happened to the best boy in my Koranic school?

MUSA: (*Moves closer.*) He grew up. And as he grew, so did his perception about life. He started to see and feel things differently. He no longer believed those little stories about right and wrong, and how Allah lived in Heaven. And how piety guaranteed us a ticket to paradise. He became amazed at the capacity of man to be evil, and wondered if God indeed lived with us on earth anymore. He grew up, Mallam, seeing the dark hearts of men. Trying to find answers to the questions of life which went beyond the innocent Islamic early alphabets in your school, Alif, baa, taa, saa! That little boy grew up.

SANI: You are angry.

MUSA: I am, Mallam. I should be! I must be!

SANI: Why?

MUSA: I stand before you a used tool for dredging water from the earth. A dreg of my grandmother's *burukutu*. A spent spirit, uncared for even by faith itself, and a living carcass ready to meet his maker.

SANI: I sense bitterness, a deep, seething melancholy in your words. May Allah …

MUSA: *Kai, Rankaidede*. Don't say one more word. It is better for me to die with you as my Koranic school teacher in my head. Rather than see pretension stand before me. (*Pause.*) You see why we kill even our own?

SANI: What?

MUSA: Why even those who call themselves spiritual fathers, leaders of the *ja ma'a*, those who wrapped their heads with well shaped *Rawani*, with well manicured fingers and beard, and know the Holy Qur'an by heart, you see why we do not spare them in the judgment of death?

SANI: No.

MUSA: Because it is better to be truthful with God. Hypocrites all! *Dukaku*!

SANI: Hypocrites. Strong words.

MUSA: (*Cynical, sarcastic.*) Not you, of course. You are a Mallam. A good man of God.

SANI: Yes. I have given my all to Almighty Allah.

MUSA: Yes. And only He can bear witness? I mean only He knows the true believer.

SANI: Yes, Son. Do not try to do Allah's work. Be careful, Son.

MUSA: Son? (*Chuckles.*) I am a product of faith. My mother died at childbirth. My grandmother brought me up. My father having died of pneumonia in my early age, my grandmother dragged me to your school as her only option.

SANI: Yes, I know all this.

MUSA: I liked your school, Sir. It was the closest to family that I knew. Your first child, Danladi, was my age mate and classmate, his father owned the school.

56

And I adopted your first wife, Hadjia Talatu, as my second mother. So while we where classified as *Almajiris,* Danladi, your son, was not. He had his hot bath, and washed his mouth. The meals we so looked forward to were his leftovers. You told us it was Allah's divine arrangement. We swallowed it, and believed you.

SANI: But it was. The fingers are not equal.

MUSA: So you said. But in the white man's school, I came first from primary one to six, your son Dandadi was always last. And yet, he got admission to go to secondary school, then university. I stopped. It was only then that your finger logic dawned on me. No one had any plans for me or my life. No one!

SANI: Yes. But the finger logic is not my creation. It belongs to Allah.

MUSA: No, it belongs to man! (*Brings out the fingers of his left hand and stares at them.*) You are indeed right, *Rankaidede*. The only solution may be to cut off the long edges and make them equal, don't you think?

SANI: Hell no!

MUSA: Don't swear, *Rankaidede*. You are a man of God.

SANI: Forgive me.

MUSA: Haa, you forget your teachings, Mallam. Only God forgives.

SANI: Yes … yes.

MUSA: And then as *Almajiris* you used us. You exploited the faith. You told us one day to burn the churches. That Allah said so. We could not doubt a man of God, so we as little boys burnt the churches.

SANI: It is such a long time ago.

MUSA: But the scars are here. To the Christians we became the devils. Satan. The prayers and songs became chants and evocations commanding their God to destroy us.

SANI: Haa!

MUSA: And since they were the ones with education, they changed the rules so much, we became excluded from our dreams. We became the wretched of the country. The unfit. Tell me, Mallam, what do dogs do when pushed to the wall even by their owners? Um? They bark and fight back. You see?

SANI: Yes ... but ...

MUSA: And politics came. And the new politicians like Danladi your son came. They promised to take us away from our failures, but instead they reminded us that we were the failures. (*Chuckles.*) They even designed special school system which would keep our cattle rearing brothers on their trail. (*Chuckles again.*) Jokers! That was when we proclaimed death to all ... (*Chuckles.*)

SANI: No one knew all these were going on inside of you. You could have spoken. A word. A sigh. Now it is all too late. Too many lives have been lost. Allah!

MUSA: *(Sighs and chuckles.)*

SANI: *(Sigh.)* All you can do is sigh? We are talking about human sanctity, and you sigh and chuckle. How sad.

MUSA: We are talking of hate for a system corrupt to the soul of those who operate it. One can taste the bitterness of hate if ... Life does not matter anymore. What matters is eternal life in the hereafter.

SANI: If only you had said a word of dialogue. An exchange of demands. A list of desires. That is how it is done. Just a word.

MUSA: A word? With who? You the clerics were busy fighting to be the leaders of the Islamic delegation to Mecca? *Amirul hajj* were more interested in making sure their great, great-grandchildren would never lack till they died. So who was going to listen to our sighs? *(Whispers.)* No one!

SANI: But the position you took is too extreme. Killing everybody. Destroying everything that stood in your way.

MUSA: No one would listen. So we had to force you. But you change your ways and all that will stop. I shall say no more.

SANI: There is so much bitterness. What do we have to do? What do I tell the Commissioner?

MUSA: Tell him that if we want to resolve this problem, we must not deceive ourselves with lies and futile promises built on deception. A genuine dialogue and peace process with the government, the people and our leaders will do it.

SANI: But they are talking with some people.

MUSA: They cannot achieve anything by talking with the wrong people.

SANI: The right people are faceless.

MUSA: You change, and the faces will appear. We are not spirits. We live among you.

(MUSA *turns his back to him.*)

SANI: (*Surprised, stares at* MUSA. *The* WARDER *moves towards* SANI, *and gestures to him to leave. Slowly he walks away.*) I shall pray for you.

(KAKA PATU *and* AMINA *come in crying and holding on to each other.* MUSA *sees them and turns his back to them.*)

PATU: Let me see your face. Let me see the face of a murderer before I die. (*She moves round to see* MUSA's *face. As she turns,* MUSA *turns. This goes on for a while.* AMINA *moves following every move by* PATU *who holds on to her. Suddenly,* PATU *lets out a wild chuckle.*) This is not the baby monster game anymore. You are no longer a child in a prittle prattle hug game with your frail grandmother, Musa. No! This is a game of death. You became a man who just won himself the prized velvet chain of death. Prepare, Son! My daughter and sister await you with your shroud.

MUSA: Take her away from here I beg you.

AMINA: What about me ... what about us? Can we go too?

PATU: Us? Huh! I have failed her! I have failed my child. No wonder she cried in her death. See how tightly he holds and wraps his new white shroud round himself like the village fool playing the role of the king of death. Heh, see how he gallops to his end, and only two of us, only two women, his poor lonely acolytes of shame to lead the masquerade to the market square.

PATU: Allah, forgive me, I failed her again.

AMINA: Who, Kaka?

PATU: My daughter. Again, and again, I fail her. Disappointed with me, she has come for him herself. She can have him. I don't know this one anymore. She can have this living carcass of my sweat.

AMINA: Kaka ... your biting words stir him.

MUSA: (*His back still turned to them, he continues to mutter.*) Guard, take these women away from me. I have finished with them.

PATU: Daughter, what did he say?

AMINA: A gibberish of his mind, coated in the foolery of his tongue. Come, Kaka, *ki bari. Mu koma gida.* Let us leave.

PATU: What did you say? (*The* WARDER *comes forward and begins to persuade them to leave.* KAKA PATU *continues to cry.*)

MUSA: *Lahilla illaha!* (MUSA *sits on the prison floor and just mutters, "Lahilla illaha" until they leave.*)

AMINA: (*As they are gently nudged out.*) Musa, you cannot do this to me! What do I do now? What do I call him, your son … our son … when he does come? Tell me. Face me and say something.

WARDER: Women, I am sorry. You must leave now.

AMINA: Don't push us. She is his grandmother. And I am … I don't even know what I am to you anymore …

WARDER: You see …

PATU: The cuckold mother of his unborn son. That is who you are, child. Only this time, death is the other woman. Pity. Let us go away from here, child.

AMINA: Yes. (*Now angry, she struggles with the* WARDER. *Returning to the cage of* MUSA's *prison.*) Talk to me, hardened man. What do I call your son? Say or I will tear him myself, limb to limb, from my womb, like you tore people from the womb of their world. Talk to me I say.

MUSA: (*Looks at her, and slowly whispers.*) Musa!

AMINA: No. Enough of that name in my life. I shall not be the vessel of doom. I will name him Abdul-Gafar … the servant of the Forgiver, and maybe then God will forgive you. (WARDER *hurries in.*)

WARDER: Woman, come. The old woman is screaming and crying. The Superintendent wants her out of here now.

AMINA: Yes, I must return to the living. The smell of death grows stronger here. (*She runs out.*)

MUSA: (*In a whisper.*) Abdul-Gafar.

WARDER: What did you say?

MUSA: Abdul-Gafar is a good name for my son. Please tell her if and when she returns. Let the Mallam whisper it into his ears at his *Sunah.*

WARDER: I shall tell her, but will she keep your child now? *A dan maraya?* A fatherless child? What story will she tell him about his father. To me, Allah forgive me. It seems so unlikely that she will keep it. (*There is a loud screech of a vehicle. Confused. Checks his watch and hurries out.*)

MUSA: (*Alone, begins to chant.*)

> *Subahanalla!*
> *Allihamdulilla!*
> *Lahilla illaha!*
>
> *Subahanalla!*
> *Allihamdulilla!*
> *Lahilla illaha!*

WARDER: (*Comes in with a covered plate of food, a cup, a bottle of soft drink. He pushes them through a wider opening in the prison cage. MUSA does not move, he continues to mutter his chant.*) Please, eat something. Tonight is going to be a short one. (*Pause.*)

They will come for you soon. That is why this treat. Rice, chicken and a drink. Liquid content only. (*Chuckles.*) The government is always generous on a night like this. (MUSA *still does not say a word.*) Shocked, eh? Not a word? Anyway they will tie you to the drum outside by the palm trees, and shoot you. (*Pause.*) I see you will still not say a word. Then when you are dead, we shall bury you in the prison graveyard not too far from here. (*Pause. Waits for* MUSA *to say something, when he does not hear a word, he shrugs his shoulders, and takes his position by the prison.* MUSA *goes on with the chant for a while, and suddenly stops.*)

MUSA: Thank you. Warder!

WARDER: (*Still standing by the prison post.*) Yes.

MUSA: My grandmother gave you a small bundle of white cloth to wrap my body. Do you still have it?

WARDER: Yes. She said it was your *likaffani*, but they won't let me use it. It will all happen so fast, a shroud will be a nicety. The soldiers don't have time for that. It is business.

MUSA: Oh.

WARDER: Oh. Don't sound like that. Eighty people died in that church. Only you survived in a manner of speaking. No one will shed a thought of kindness on your body. The Superintendent's uncle was one of those who died. He has brought out the acid bottle. Even your bones will be dissolved by noon tomorrow. Just prepare to meet your God.

MUSA: Which God? I was not supposed to be alive. I was told it was all to be in a flash. I call God, a flash, a loud bang, and stillness in tattered shreds. Fast as a flash. Now which God do I face when the bullet touches my skin, and pierces my heart? Which God will come to receive me? Um?

WARDER: Eat something. You need the strength to meet whoever comes for you in the world beyond. Eat, I beg you. (*He watches as* MUSA *goes to the bowl opens it, and closes it again.*) Not even a mouthful?

MUSA: No. What am I eating for? My life all washed off! Nothing has come out of it.

WARDER: Em ... if this will cheer you up, you are a hero you know. A bad one, but a hero all the same.

MUSA: A hero. (*Chuckles.*)

WARDER: Yes. It was the way you went about it. The general condition in the country was indeed very bad. The government, the people, everybody was bad. Corruption reigned supreme. Yes. But you started killing everybody. And we got confused. Even your own people. And so we started willing your downfall, your end.

MUSA: Um.

WARDER: Who will cry for you tomorrow in the government blanket half-ridden with rat holes from the kit room? Who?

MUSA: We failed then?

WARDER: No. I have not said so. I only said ... If you had

called the country to order in some other ways than death. If only …

MUSA: No … no more. Indeed you have said enough to put a doubt even in the heart of stones we were trained to have. Your country was so bad.

WARDER: Yes, we know, but was your solution the right one? Was your way the right way?

MUSA: (*Excited.*) But we showed you hell all the same, eh? The only thing you people fear is death, so we allowed you to meet it. We did it the best way we could.

WARDER: Yes, that is why you must be allowed to die like a common thief caught with a gun. I shall cover you with some honour tonight.

MUSA: How? Run away? To where? How far?

WARDER: Slip away. Through the hands and watchful eyes and tips of the bayonets of death.

MUSA: How?

WARDER: I have rat poison here in my pocket. I bought it for the rats in my house.

MUSA: So?

WARDER: Let me add a little to your drink. And spare you the pinch of the bullet. The death will be instant. Please consider my offer. (*Sound of soldiers from backstage.*)

MUSA: Mix it. Quick. The footsteps grow impatient.

WARDER: (*Opens the bottle of drink, he pours the medicine which he takes from his pocket into the bottle. There is a call of the* WARDER *from back stage.*) Sir! Here! (*Gives the bottle to* MUSA.) The Superintendent calls. They only have one armed robber tonight, then you. Do it now. If God decided to show you some mercy, this may be it. Be a man. (*He hurries out.*)

MUSA: Be a man ... I am a man ... but I think I haggled too long with death, so now I shall die a fool's death. Oh my spirit is restless. But my heart is in search of sense, melts. Pity. (*More sounds of soldiers' movements. Slowly* MUSA *lifts the bottle to his mouth. He stops, looks around. Sounds of gunshots.*) Now my turn approaches. Um. (*He makes up his mind, as he lifts the bottle to his mouth, again he stops, hesitant. The sound of soldiers marching is heard.*) Death is here. Alhamdullilahi!

(*Slowly final lights fade.*)

THE END.

Kraftgriots

Also in the series (DRAMA) *(continued)*

Emmanuel Emasealu: *The Gardeners* (2008)
Emmanuel Emasealu (ed.) *The CRAB Plays I* (2008)
Emmanuel Emasealu (ed.) *The CRAB Plays II* (2008)
Richard Ovuorho: *Reaping the Whirlwind* (2008)
Sam Ukala: *Two plays* (2008)
Ahmed Yerima: *Akuabata* (2008)
Ahmed Yerima: *Tuti* (2008)
Niyi Adebanjo: *Two Plays: A Market of Betrayals & A Monologue on the Dunghill* (2008)
Chris Anyokwu: *Homecoming* (2008)
Ahmed Yerima: *Mojagbe* (2009)
Ahmed Yerima: *The Ife Quartet* (2009)
'Muyiwa Ojo: *Memoirs of a Lunatic* (2009)
John Iwuh: *Spellbound* (2009)
Osita C. Ezenwanebe: *Dawn of Full Moon* (2009)
Ahmed Yerima: *Dami's Cross & Atika's Well* (2009)
Osita C. Ezenwanebe: *Giddy Festival* (2009)
Peter Omoko: *Battles of Pleasure* (2009)
Ahmed Yerima: *Little Drops ...* (2009)
Arnold Udoka: *Long Walk to a Dream* (2009), winner, 2010 ANA/NDDC J.P. Clark drama prize
Arnold Udoka: *Inyene: A Dance Drama* (2009)
Chris Anyokwu: *Termites* (2010)
Julie Okoh: *A Haunting Past* (2010)
Arnold Udoka: *Mbarra: A Dance Drama* (2010)
Chukwuma Anyanwu: *Another Weekend, Gone!* (2010)
Oluseyi Adigun: *Omo Humuani: Abubaka Olusola Saraki, Royal Knight of Kwara* (2010)
Eni Jologho Umuko: *The Scent of Crude Oil* (2010)
Olu Obafemi: *Ogidi Mandate* (2010), winner, 2011 ANA/NDDC J.P. Clark drama prize
Ahmed Yerima: *Ajagunmale* (2010)
Ben Binebai: *Drums of the Delta* (2010)
'Diran Ademiju-Bepo: *Rape of the Last Sultan* (2010)
Chris Iyimoga: *Son of a Chief* (2010)
Arnold Udoka: *Rainbow Over the Niger & Nigeriana* (2010)
Julie Okoh: *Our Wife Forever* (2010)
Barclays Ayakoroma: *A Matter of Honour* (2010)
Barclays Ayakoroma: *Dance on His Grave* (2010)
Isiaka Aliagan: *Olubu* (2010)
Ahmed Yerima: *Mu'adhin's Call* (2011)
Emmanuel Emasealu: *Nerves* (2011)

68

Alex Roy-Omoni: *The Ugly Ones* (2011)
Osita Ezenwanebe: *Adaugo* (2011)
Osita Ezenwanebe: *Daring Destiny* (2011)
Ahmed Yerima: *No Pennies for Mama* (2011)
Ahmed Yerima: *Mu'adhin's Call* (2011)
Barclays Ayakoroma: *A Chance to Survive and Other Plays* (2011)
Barclays Ayakoroma: *Castles in the Air* (2011)
Arnold Udoka: *Akon* (2011)
Arnold Udoka: *Still Another Night* (2011)
Sunnie Ododo: *Hard Choice* (2011)
Sam Ukala: *Akpakaland and Other Plays* (2011)
Greg Mbajiorgu: *Wake Up Everyone!* (2011)
Ahmed Yerima: *Three Plays* (2011)
Ahmed Yerima: *Igatibi* (2012)
Esanmabeke Opuofeni: *Song of the Gods* (2012)
Karo Okokoh: *Teardrops of the Gods* (2012)
Esanmabeke Opuofeni: *The Burning House* (2012)
Dan Omatsola: *Olukume* (2012)
Alex Roy-Omoni: *Morontonu* (2012)
Dauda Enna: *Banquet of Treachery* (2012)
Chinyere G. Okafor: *New Toyi-Toyi* (2012)
Greg Mbajiorgu: *The Prime Minister's Son* (2012)
Karo Okokoh: *Sunset So Soon* (2012)
Sunnie Ododo: *Two Liberetti: To Return from the Void & Vanishing Vapour* (2012)
Gabriel B. Egbe: *Emani* (2013)
Isiaka Aliagan: *Oba Mama* (2013)
Shehu Sani: *When Clerics Kill* (2013)
Ahmed Yerima: *Tafida & Other Plays* (2013)
Osita Ezenwanebe: *Shadows on Arrival* (2013)
Praise C. Daniel-Inim: *Married But Single and Other plays* (2013)
Bosede Ademilua-Afolayan: *Look Back in Gratitude* (2013)
Greg Mbajiorgu: *Beyond the Golden Prize* (2013)